T0360941

Routledge Revivals

Uplift in Economics

First published in 1929, *Uplift in Economics* is a self-proclaimed propaganda against the influence of moral judgement in social science research. The author argues that while the development of mankind is an honourable goal of economics and political science, the understanding and the execution of such development should not be marred by the moral beliefs of the researcher. Instead, priority should be given to scientific temper and empirical facts while carrying out any research. Over the years, the binary of reason and feeling has been replaced with a negotiation of the two; however, it is interesting to study the treatment of this debate at various points in history. This book will be of interest to students of economics, political science, psychology, philosophy and history.

Uplift in Economics

A Plea for the Exclusion of Moral Implications from
Economics and the Political Sciences

P. Sargant Florence

Routledge
Taylor & Francis Group

First published in 1929
by Kegan Paul, Trench, Trubner & Co. Ltd

This edition first published in 2022 by Routledge
4 Park Square, Milton Park, Abingdon, Oxon, OX14 4RN
and by Routledge
605 Third Avenue, New York, NY 10017

Routledge is an imprint of the Taylor & Francis Group, an informa business

Publisher's Note
The publisher has gone to great lengths to ensure the quality of this reprint but points
out that some imperfections in the original copies may be apparent.

Disclaimer
The publisher has made every effort to trace copyright holders and welcomes
correspondence from those they have been unable to contact.

A Library of Congress record exists under LCCN: 34003463

ISBN: 978-1-032-30782-4 (hbk)
ISBN: 978-1-003-30680-1 (ebk)
ISBN: 978-1-032-30812-8 (pbk)

Book DOI 10.4324/9781003306801

UPLIFT
IN ECONOMICS

A Plea for the Exclusion of Moral Implications
from Economics and the Political Sciences

BY

P. SARGANT FLORENCE,

Professor of Commerce in the University of Birmingham.
Late Lecturer in Economics and Politics in the University of Cambridge.
Author of "Economics of Fatigue and Unrest," "Over-population,"
"Economics and Human Behaviour," "The Statistical Method in
Economics and Political Science."

LONDON
KEGAN PAUL, TRENCH, TRUBNER & Co., Ltd.
BROADWAY HOUSE, CARTER LANE, E.C.
1929

Printed in Great Britain by
R. I. SEVERS. CAMBRIDGE

CONTENTS

PROLOGUE

This essay is, frankly, propaganda. But the doctrine to be propagated is that economics and the political and social sciences should eschew propaganda.

Whatever their conduct as private persons or as educators with the full allowance of human emotions and sentiments, there should at least be some economists, political scientists and sociologists who will devote themselves to research and will take their studies as seriously as do physicists, biologists or anthropologists, and who, however keen to improve the lot of man and *lift him upward*, will be content to confine their conclusions within the scientific stage of that process of uplift.

§ 1
STEPS IN SCIENTIFIC UPLIFT

In a paper read in 1913 before the Cambridge " Heretics " I distinguished three distinct steps or stages—a sort of practical syllogism—in the deliberate or " purposive " process of applying scientific knowledge, whether political, economic or biological, for the good and uplift of mankind.

" In a recent number of one of our kaleidoscopic magazines " I observed, " there appeared written in large type the following pathetic injunction : *Kill that Fly*, and underneath, in smaller type, *Why? One Fly may carry and distribute millions of germs of typhoid and diptheria, etc.*"

" This " I continued " is a clear case of the Purposive Application of Knowledge to Life :

The Knowledge here, is that one fly may carry certain diseases.

9

UPLIFT IN ECONOMICS

The Purpose is to abolish disease.

The Application of knowledge to the purpose is " Kill that fly ".

Three different elements can thus be distinguished in the whole application.

1. The Knowledge.

2. The Purpose.

3. The Policy or Practice advocated in life."

I would not have the temerity to publish these observations within the field of moral science made in early youth, if I had not subsequently read Dr. Neville Keynes' formulation of the threefold distinction between economic uniformities, economic ideals, and economic precepts.[1]

"When we leave the enquiry into the veritable order of economic phenomena, their co-existences and sequences, under existing or assumed conditions, we still have to take account of a further subdivision of some significance. There is, on the one hand, the investigation of economic ideals and the determination of a standard by reference to which the social worth of economic activities and

[1] *Scope and Method of Political Economy*, p. 32.

conditions may be judged ; and there is also the investigation of economic rules, i.e. the determination of maxims or precepts by obedience to which given ends may best be obtained ".

The first two steps of this " practical syllogism ", the knowledge of the " veritable order of phenomena ", and the purpose or ideal in view, are independent in the sense that any particular piece of knowledge may be associated with any of a variety of particular purposes. In the next Great War to End War we may well be using the knowledge that flies spread disease, not to avoid disease, but to spread it among those who happen to be our enemies for the time being ; such a plan was proposed as early as 1763 by the British Commander in Chief in America, who suggested spreading smallpox germs in order to exterminate Indian border tribes.[1]

The first two steps are equally necessary for any practical policy to be logically justified and should strictly speaking be regarded as simultaneous premisses. The

[1] Cox, *Life of Bishop Colenso*, Appendix F.

second step might have been quoted first, the first second; but the third step, the precept or practice recommended, is always dependent upon, and must follow, the other two.

I proceeded to argue, before the " Heretics ", that each of the three steps is undertaken in a different spirit; and that the differences were most clearly expressed in the various " moods " distinguished by grammarians. The first step should always be capable of expression in the Indicative (or Subjunctive) Mood, the second in the Optative Mood, and the third in the Imperative. Actually, the indicative (or subjunctive) mood coupled with some synonym (adjective or substantive) of good or bad, may take the place of the optative and also of the imperative mood; and in any case of course, the optative and imperative are usually expressed in English by the help of auxiliary verbs. We can say instead of " kill that fly ", it is good to kill flies or flies ought to be killed; and instead of " would that there were no disease ! " we can say " disease is bad " or " disease is a nuisance ".

STEPS IN SCIENTIFIC UPLIFT

In the typical case the first step, or "indicative premiss", is a more or less scientific statement or law of coexistences or sequences, involving usually, some relationship of cause and effect ; the second step, or optative premiss, expresses a desire for, or abhorrence of, the effect indicated in the first step ; and the third step "applies" the scientific statement in order to establish the effect desired, to lift things the desired "upward" direction, or else to prevent the effect abhorred and a falling downward into sin.

The scientific law in the indicative mood may well be a statement of what various people think ought to be. A "fact" in law "includes the fact that any mental condition of which any person is conscious exists ".[1] Thus it is a statement of fact in Economics that some people think sweated trades ought to be discouraged, and refuse to buy the products of these trades. The main clause of the sentence "many purchasers think sweating ought to be discouraged"

[1] Stephen, *Digest of the Law of Evidence*, p. 1.

remains in the indicative mood in the letter as well as the spirit. This point would not need reiteration if economists did not write confusedly about it still. In his *Supply and Demand* Henderson mentions[2] that "we are sometimes advised to distinguish sharply between 'What should be and What is'", but meets this by arguing that "our sense of 'what should be' reacts upon 'what is'". In these two passages "we" or "our" refers to quite different persons, or to the same persons in quite different capacities. The advice is sound for the student and observer of human reactions, but it is not *his* sense of what should be that will react upon what is, but the observee's, the observed re-agent's, sense. Sir Josiah Stamp is, however, clear enough. "Since what people think, however unjustifiably or erroneously, affects their conduct and motives, and has, therefore, economic significance, these ideas are, as existing features of conduct, economic *facts* or ingredients".

The desire or abhorrence expressed in

[2] Chapter IX, § 2.

14

STEPS IN SCIENTIFIC UPLIFT

the optative stage is probably *ultimately* based on some instinctive emotion, moral judgment or *sense of sin*, though in any given practical syllogism it is usually derived from some logically antecedent or ulterior syllogism. The effect is desired or abhorred, because it has been, or could be, indicated as the cause of some ulterior effect desired or abhorred.

I may object to disease not in itself but because experience has previously indicated to me that it is painful and I am in no (optative) mood for pain. In this case the basis of the second step of the original syllogism is rationally *derived* from the two premisses of an antecedent syllogism; it is in fact a repetition of the third step of an antecedent practical syllogism. If the optative step is placed first instead of second, the chain of reasoning can be visualized by capitalizing and italicizing the antecedent syllogism whose imperative becomes the succeeding syllogism's optative, and by heading the steps Opt : for Optative, Ind : for Indicative, Imp : for Imperative.

15

UPLIFT IN ECONOMICS

Opt : Oh That I May Not Suffer
Pain.

Ind : Disease is Painful.

Imp : Let Us Prevent Disease.

= Opt : *Oh that there may be no disease.*

Ind : *Flies carry disease.*

Imp : *Kill that fly.*

= Opt : Oh that flies might be killed.

Ind : Swatting kills flies faster than other means.

Imp : Let us then secure fly-swatters.

= Opt : Oh that we may secure fly-swatters.

Etc., etc.

Take a practical syllogism of more serious import, written in the original order of steps.

Ind : A high standard of living results in greater restraint in the creation of children.

Opt : Oh that there were more restraint in the creation of children !

Imp : Let us encourage a high standard of living.

16

STEPS IN SCIENTIFIC UPLIFT

The optative premiss may not be based on any emotional objection to children or life as such, but might simply be uttered by one who (however naturally philoprogenitive) was convinced by the teaching of Malthus, and believed firmly in the " law of diminishing return ". Yet Malthus' doctrine depends ultimately on some emotional feeling or ethical judgment, such as objection to vice, misery or pain, as much as did our objection to disease. The chain of causes and effects may stretch far back, but *ultimately* must be attached to some quite irrational or non-rational anchor digging deep into our " human nature ". Those who favour large populations and a high birth rate, and they appear to be in a majority, may well admit Malthus' indicative statements as a fact and yet prefer large numbers to the mere avoidance of individual vice and misery. They may be obedient subjects to some Moral law, or else believers in national power, or they may believe that a maximum sum of happiness is better than a maximum average of happiness per head.

UPLIFT IN ECONOMICS

In every case the optative toward which the practical policy adopted or advocated is aimed (i.e. the " up " in uplift), or away from which that policy flees, as from sin, is ultimately a matter of personal emotion or judgment, independent of the indicative statement of fact ; thus men with quite divergent optative " outlooks " should find it possible to find agreement in their indicative observation and interpretation of the facts. The compounding of the optative mood into statements of fact, and constant introduction of the imperative, thus leads, as we shall see, to unnecessary disagreement and confusion.

§ 2

THE CASE AGAINST MORAL IMPLICATIONS

The embryonic and parlous state of Economics, Political Science, and Sociology generally is probably due more to the admixture of moral implication with scientific observation than to any other cause. There are at least three ways in which moral implications—ideals about social service and sin—obstruct and confound learning :

(a) The writer's moral outlook—his ideals of what is " up "—may not tally with those of the reader, and if the author mixes up that outlook with his statement of fact, the latter, though perfectly true, may be rejected or resisted along with the former as mere propaganda. However intelligible the writer's scientific conclusions, his " foreign " ethical code or his strange sense of sin will be a source of distraction, and communication with

19

his audience will be entirely or partially baulked by his peculiar desires and moral ideals.

(*b*) Admixture with moral outlook may render statements of facts unintelligible to the audience. When some action is considered desirable and called good, high, or uplifting, conducive, in short to the fulfilment of the writer's peculiar plans and desires, the reader or communicant generally may remain ignorant of the precise nature of the desires referred to and, probably, will unconsciously suppose that what he (the communi*cant*) happens to consider desirable and uplifting is what the communicator is referring to by good, etc. Here communication with his audience is vitiated by the author's ideals and moralizings being *misunderstood* and the audience misled.

(*c*) As a result of compounding moral considerations of uplift with a purely indicative attitude the author may actually mislead and confuse himself. If the words he uses have an ethical colour, they are likely to be indefinite

MORAL IMPLICATIONS

and ambiguous enough to change in meaning in different contexts ; and if the author enunciates " principles " that might be indicative *or* optative *or* imperative in mood he may deduce fiction from them rather than fact.

Each of these sources of obstruction and confusion will be considered in consecutive sections.

§ 3

THE AUDIENCE DISTRACTED

" Because in economic theory ", writes Dr. Keynes,[1] " men's action in buying and selling is commonly assumed to be governed by self-interest, political economy is supposed to inculcate selfishness ". And continual reference to thrifty workpeople, to alert business men such as the speculative ferry-man or jerry-builder, and to the provident consumer,[2] make these persons appear almost as heroes in the economists' eyes however unpleasant they prove to be when encountered in real life, or when their works are contemplated aesthetically. The mere knowledge that an author is an economist usually antagonises the general reader and queers the pitch at

[1] J. N. Keynes, *Scope and Method of Political Economy*, p. 50.

[2] e.g. Marshall, *Principles of Economics*, 6th Ed., pp. 117, 118, 358, 438, etc.

22

THE AUDIENCE DISTRACTED

the outset ;[1] and economists must certainly
be on their guard against inculcating
any so-called materialist outlook or
implying what are generally called materialist precepts. But this possible bias
on the part of the economist is no more
peculiar to him, and contrary to that
of his audience, than that of profession-
ally interested experts in other branches
of social research.

Suppose an imperial government has
built roads in the territory of a more or
less savage tribe and expects to be
repaid, but that the taxes they have
decreed have not been forthcoming.

A military expert reporting to the
Cabinet may be impressed by a general's
resource in using aeroplanes to subdue
recalcitrant tribesmen, and his argument
reduced to the practical syllogism might
run :

Ind : Bombs dropped from aeroplanes
soon bring savages to heel.

Opt : Savages must be made to pay
their taxes.

[1] Economics is still spoken of as the " dismal
science ". See my *Economics and Human
Behaviour*, § III.

UPLIFT IN ECONOMICS

Imp : Use bombs dropped from aeroplanes.

But the responsible statesman, in touch with other considerations besides the economic or military, might not consider the militarist's imperative as suitable, or his optative as final and enshrining an ideal to be obtained at the costs of all other sentiments.

The military expert should confine himself to his *indicative* statement ; his optative sentiments and the imperative policy that rests upon this optative are irrelevant. And by making these irrelevant remarks that are *ultra vires*—beyond his ken—he jeopardises the acceptance of his perfectly correct indicative statement as to a most effective method of *causing* the specific *result* of bringing tribesmen to heel.

Later on, let us suppose, a diplomatic expert with a pacifist tinge is sent among the tax-defaulting tribesmen. He is impressed by the pride of a chief on receiving an Imperial title such as the Knighthood of the Garter, and might find that in return the chief was prepared to give an

24

elephant a year as a " gift " to his paramount Over-lord, equivalent in value to
the taxes that might be extracted by
bombs.

The diplomat might then be tempted
to " syllogise " as follows :

Ind : Knighthoods of the Garter granted
to tribal potentates elicit in " gifts "
the equivalent of taxes.

Opt : Savages must be made to pay
toward road-building in their territory.

Imp : Shower potentates with garters
not bombs.

But here again, though this diplomatic
expert's *observation* of fact was perfectly
correct—and pyschologically most interesting—it does not follow that his optative
or his imperative will be accepted.
Responsible statesmen may have a
feeling against cheapening knighthoods
of the garter and may think it almost
as sinful as the sale of honours at home.
And, as in the case of the militarist without
the milk of human kindness, the rejection
of the optative and imperative of the
pacifist without honour will probably
involve the rejection and pigeon-holing

of his perfectly valid and important indicative observation.

The judgment—the optative and imperative—of the scientific expert or specialist is not necessarily ultimate and final, and when he advances them as such his reader or client is justified in withstanding his authority. No practical policies can be determined solely from the study of one branch of social research such as economics, or indeed from the study of sociology as a whole apart from some optative premiss. But the optative of the specialist whether *qua* specialist or *qua* an ordinary man can seldom form an adequate basis for action. The scientist had therefore best devote himself to the observation of coexistences, sequences, and causes and effects, without pronouncing which is the *desirable* existence, sequel or effect, or how to obtain that specific desideratum of his.

When the communication of thought consists in teaching rather than the advising of government the temptation to moralize is perhaps greater ; but since the indicative findings are, in that case,

THE AUDIENCE DISTRACTED

not confined to the causation of given
results (e.g. getting a revenue) but may
also discuss the consequences of given
causes, the effects of distracting the
audience is yet more disastrous to the
development of a science.

In text-books used for teaching, the
" critical " method of discussing some
social institution or some human course
of action is very popular. A list of the
several " advantages " and " disadvantages " (or pros and cons, merits and
defects, benefits and dangers, etc.) of
the course of action or institution is
often put before the pupil. Both advantages and disadvantages (and the various
synonyms of the two) are presumably
all *results* of the institution or course of
action, and the distinction may differ-
entiate between these results in a somewhat arbitrary way, depending entirely
upon the author's private point of view,
his criterion of virtue or sin. A reader
may agree about some results being
advantageous but disagree about the
advantageousness of other results which
the author proceeds roundly also to

call advantages. And this disagreement between author and audience may break off their relations. The reader or auditor exclaims that the author is wrong-headed and the author's audience diminishes by one—which is a pity, for the author was perhaps only wrong-hearted.

The author may have made an important scientific discovery about some result following the course of action or institution he was discussing. Had he called that result neither an advantage nor a disadvantage, had he regarded the institution or course of action neither as potentially meritorious or potentially sinful, *all* his audience might have followed him and might have advanced in learning.

Even if the alien sense of sin of the writer or expert, the " communicator ", does not condemn him as entirely wrong-headed in the mind of his reader or client, it may tend to " put off " the communicant or fill him with extraneous emotions sufficiently strong to prevent his reception and adoption of the thought communicated. This unfortunate effect often takes place, I believe, among certain of

or of things as unfortunate or scandalous that tend toward the foreign reader's satisfaction. Adjectives implying neither sadness or rejoicing can certainly be found that will refer successfully to whatever the writer really wants to indicate.

The education of the more serious and morally earnest members of the English ruling (and writing) class is peculiarly influenced by the ideas of Thomas Arnold, so that Englishmen should be particularly on their guard in this matter when they realize Arnold's private views of, say, Frenchmen. Here is an extract from his travelling journal dated Joigny, April 6th, 1827.[1]

" I have been struck with the total absence of all gentlemen, and of all persons of the education and feelings of gentlemen. I am afraid that the bulk of the people are sadly ignorant and unprincipled. . . . May He, who only can, turn the hearts of this people, and of all other people, to the knowledge and love of Himself in His Son. . . . And

[1] Stanley's *Life of Arnold*, Appendix **D.**

may He keep alive in me the spirit of charity, to judge favourably and feel kindly towards those amongst whom I am travelling ; inasmuch as Christ died for them as well as for us, and they too call themselves after His name ".

These criticisms may seem cantankerous, yet it is essential, for teaching and communicating purposes, that the writer on social questions shall remain *en rapport* with his audience and shall not cause distraction or irritation superfluous and irrelevant to the communication of his thought.

When the audience consists of fellow authors in the same field of research the danger incurred by introducing distracting ethical notions is still more patent. Each fellow author may believe in a different criterion of right and wrong and may spend his life in crushing the criterion and with it the scientific theories of his predecessors.   His own criterion and theory will then be crushed up and the crusher crushed . . . ad infinitum.

Trouble might be saved if the scientific knowledge conveyed were detached from any criterion of good. If writers were content to state the facts, general or particular, without obtruding their view of what is upward or their conception of sin, a body of knowledge might be formed by their united efforts which might be of use to men with all sorts of views.

" What ", asks Bagehot, in his *Physics and Politics*, " is progress, and what is decline ? Even in the animal world there is no applicable rule accepted by physiologists, which settles what animals are higher or lower than others ; there are controversies about it. Still more then in the more complex combinations and politics of human beings it is likely to be hard to find an agreed criterion for saying which nation is before another, or what age of a nation was marching forward and which was falling back. Archbishop Manning would have one rule of progress and decline ; Professor Huxley, in most important points, quite an opposite rule ; what one would set down as an advance, the other would set down as a retreat. Each has a distinct

33

B

end which he wishes and a distinct calamity which he fears, but the desire of the one is pretty near the fear of the other; books would not hold the controversy between them. Again, in art, who is to settle what is advance and what decline? Would Mr. Ruskin agree with anyone else on this subject, would he even agree with himself or could any common enquirer venture to say whether he was right or wrong? I am afraid that I must, as Sir Wm. Hamilton used to say, ' truncate a problem which I cannot solve '. I must decline to sit in judgment on disputed points of art, morals, or religion ".

Scholars will agree about the truth of a thing when they will not agree about its goodness. Let them therefore unite in discovering the truth and limit quarrelling and distracting one another about good, to the minimum amount apparently necessary for the health of the ordinary normal person. For in these matters of " ethics " their views need carry no more weight than those of " mere " laymen of similar general experience of life and of similar native

THE AUDIENCE DISTRACTED

discrimination and judgment of values. Scientists will not waste their special talents in premature applications of their findings, but will do their bit in putting facts, theories and conclusions at the disposal of the public. The result will be not less public discussion of the rights and wrongs of social conditions, but a less distracted, better defined and better-informed discussion.

§ 4

THE AUDIENCE MISLED

" No one would claim that the emancipation of woman, in the sense of freeing her from those things which have prevented the highest and best development of her personality, is not desirable. But this emancipation of woman has brought with it certain opportunities for going down as well as for going up. Woman's emancipation has not, in other words, meant to all classes of women, woman's elevation. On the contrary, it has been to some, if not an opportunity for licence, at least an opportunity for self-assertion and selfishness not consistent with the welfare of society and particularly with the stability of the family. We may remind ourselves . . . that the Roman women achieved complete emancipation, but they did not thereby better their social position. On the contrary, the emancipation of woman

THE AUDIENCE MISLED

in Rome meant woman's degradation, and ultimately the demoralization of Roman family life. While this is not necessarily an accompaniment of woman's emancipation, still it is a real danger which threatens, and of which we can already see many evidences in modern society. As in all other emancipatory movements, the dangers of freedom are found for some individuals at least to be quite as great as the dangers of subjection ".

In this short paragraph from a standard American text-book of sociology,[1] the exact references of the words highest, best (or better), desirable, up, down, elevation, degradation, welfare, demoralization, danger, seem to me difficult to discover without knowing the author's point of view and up-bringing. There are no introductory chapters of definitions, no glossary attached to the book that would interpret the words to one not in the author's immediate circle ; and I defy any such outsider to discover from this passage what is the exact information which the writer wished to convey.

[1] Ellwood, *Sociology and Modern Social Problems*, p. 124-5.

UPLIFT IN ECONOMICS

If the reader's mind remained a vacuum it would not so much matter; but nature, we are told, abhors a vacuum and all sorts of new emotions and old "engrams" (as engraved in childhood under terms such as sacred, wicked, naughty) will rush into his mind as being the things referred to by any of the "right-and-wrong" order of words. Vistas of his own ideals will open up in the reader's mind; yet the views disclosed would possibly be unintelligible to the author, or if intelligible might well be horrifying. Suppose one of Professor Ellwood's readers were a Mahomedan? He could cordially agree with all of Professor Ellwood's paragraph, yet what meanings would he not read into the "stability of the family" and "bettering woman's social position"!

Audiences are usually only too eager to find a "moral" in what they read or hear, that was never intended. When he delivered his Presidential Address on *Population and Unemployment* to the Economic Section of the British Association in 1922, did Sir William Beveridge

THE AUDIENCE MISLED

intend to imply all that the press comments " read " into his words ?[1] Authorities on social questions are admittedly hard put to it, however scientific they may wish to be, for some words almost *have* to be used, which to men in the street have a moral significance. Thus when a political scientist[2] states that " nominated second chambers are generally weak ", it is immediately concluded by the public that he is condemning such nominated chambers. Weakness carries some sense of " bad " (the words the German uses for bad are " schlimm " and " schlecht " corresponding etymologically to our slim and slight). Whereas, if the political scientist was worthy the name, he was neither condemning nor praising second chambers but merely making an interesting generalization about their functioning and powers. To free their science from ethical adulteration, sociologists, therefore, must not

[1] In his " Reply " Mr. Keynes appends a number of these comments. Cf. *Economic Journal*, December, 1923.

[2] e.g. H.W.C. Temperley, *Senates and Upper Chambers*.

only approach their subject in the indicative mood but must show their readers that they are doing so. Should words not morally significant fail them, they must explicitly proclaim the independence of their attitude, or else abandon idiom and syntax in favour of geometric diagram, analytic chart, acrostic tables, or a technical quasi-algebraic language of technical symbols.

Writers, if they are going to use loose, doctrinal words like moral, immoral, and any of the seventeen adjectives synonymous with right, or the twenty-one adjectives synonymous with wrong, or any of the thirty-five synonyms of virtuous or of the hundred and twenty nine synonyms of vicious[1] must make

[1] Adjectives only. Roget's *Thesaurus*, Sections 944-5 and 648-9. Further synonyms may also be found listed under Good Man (948) and Bad Man (949). The lavish wealth of the language in this respect speaks strongly for the English moral sense, if it is not positive prudishness and fear of using good old-fashioned abuse such as sluttish, scurvy, bawdy, reechy, reasty, etc. The greater number of synonyms (many of them quite discarded) for bad, vicious, and wrong than for good virtuous and right would suggest prudishness rather than love of virtue.

clear what it is they consider moral, good
or virtuous, i.e. they must definitely
publish the second (optative) premiss
of the " practical " syllogism.

This is Professor Pigou's plan in his
Economics of Welfare. The maximum
and most regular and equally distributed
National Dividend possible, is taken as
the end desired and everything is judged
by its effect on that end. This end is
objective and measurable ;[1] and if the
reader substitutes in his mind some such
phrase as " conducive to or successful
in increasing, regularizing (over time), and
equally distributing (over persons) the
National Dividend ", wherever Professor
Pigou uses words of approval without
this " specification ", there should be no
misinterpretation.

Peirce has suggested that the long
phrases, which must continually recur
if the author is to be indicative yet
explicit, might be referred to (in the
manner now familar to students of
Russian institutions) by one word, com-

---

[1] Except where a " Real " National Dividend
is recognized as differing from the *Money*
Dividend.

posed of the first letters of all the words in the phrase. Thus, instead of good Pigou might use, or his reader might bear in mind, the word IREND—Increasing, Regularizing and Equally-distributing the National Dividend—or IND, where it is only the Increase of the N.D. that is referred to.

The convenience of using a word or two instead of a whole phrase is obvious, and morally-toned words are, I admit, particularly short, spicy and convenient. Moreover, if and when the reader has grasped what the author refers to by " good ", allusions to good or bad and their various degrees and synonyms, enable him to orientate his thoughts when reading, just as the convention that the bottom of a map shall refer to the South makes it simpler to think of the various directions by thinking of South as downward and the other quarters as upward, to right, and to left respectively. Yet the use of words with moral implications however carefully their reference is expounded from the beginning, carries many dangers. The reader may

42

at any moment stray back to his own or to the popular system of rights and wrongs.

It is for this reason particularly difficult for writers who do not accept current doctrines to make headway, unless they heave overboard these fly-paper words to which have been stuck emotions other than those which the writers wish to catch. A " satisfactory " birth-rate would probably convey to the man in the street a *higher* rather than a *lower* proportion of births to population, and however clearly they may have defined at the outset what is satisfactory to them, it is advisable for Malthusians if they wish to make their statements intelligible, not to use 'satisfactory' or any of its synonyms too many pages away from the original definition. The propaganda of the Mercantilists has made a " favourable " balance of trade almost a technical phrase indicating a surplus of visible exports over imports ; and those who find imports as favourable to a country's prosperity as its exports must avoid using the adjective if they

would be understood. Similarly with
" sound " monetary policy, which usually
refers to the absence of inflation or even
to deflation. The very word inflation
or inflationist is now used as a term of
abuse and synonymous with unsound ;
and if inflationist, the expert cannot
praise his views as " sound " without
every likelihood of misunderstanding.

More open to misunderstanding than mere
synonyms of right and wrong, are words
that once had a specific " indicative "
reference but which, by continual propaganda and indoctrination on the part of
particular schools of thought, have
become generally accepted as equivalent
to good (or bad) in some respects, if not
good (or bad) in all respects. Religious,
patriotic, idealistic, constructive, noble,
productive, natural or true to one's
higher nature, on the one hand ; material-
istic, suggestive, destructive, sceptical,
on the other, are commonly used as
synonymous with *good* or *bad* respectively,
and it would be more economical of
words and more intelligible, if those
crude but simple and straightforward

adjectives were substituted. The reader
would then have more chance or realizing
that the writers particular idea of right
was indicated and would not be confused
by knowing—if he is sophisticated— the
specific and often peculiar notions of
what is right involved in most forms of
religions, national codes of honour, or
systems of ideals generally. Besides, the
more intelligent reader or auditor may
not think every form of patriotism,
religion, idealism to be necessarily always
right or every form of materialism, etc.,
always wrong. It ought to be possible
to indicate the specific reference of these
sentiments or philosophies without dealing
out praise or blame each time. The
author should search for neutral words
which, like temperature implying neither
hot nor cold,[1] imply qualities neither
good nor bad.

Many compound words, with ethical
as well as indicative implications are
also, it should be noted, incomplete. To
be productive is usually considered good,

[1] Though, to be sure " to have a temperature "
means a temperature over 98°.

45

though it may not appear so to the sweated producer. But in any case the adjective does not tell the reader the nature of the product, any more than the adjective idealistic tells him what are the ideals followed. Overcome by the emotional power of those words the reader dives off the deep end without further enquiry as to the precise reference that is indicated, and hears no more. He has definitely plunged " for " or " against ", and is deaf to all accurate and indicative specifications.

§ 5

THE AUTHOR SELF-CONFOUNDED

If readers object to, are put off by, or misunderstand the author's language it might be considered their own "look-out". *Caveat lector*. It is the author's own train of thought that matters and he cannot object to his own moral system or be put off by it, or misunderstand it.

This supposition seems on first sight reasonable, yet Spencer in his *Study of Sociology* devotes five successive chapters to various types of bias that tend to vitiate an author's conclusions; and he illustrates under each head the subjective and emotional difficulties, passions, likings and repugnances that hinder knowledge among scientists if they hold particular *educational, patriotic, class, political* or *theological* ideals. And apart from these possibly inborn and inbred types of bias many writers seem to acquire a peculiar author's bias in over-estimating the effect of the particular factors they are dealing with. A historian of the old school from over-much reading and writing of battles and warfare and their immediate effects —unaccompanied by any healthy release in the real thing—is likely to become an ardent believer in the efficacy of arms in determining the general course of history. And an economist, through his study of the " delicate mechanism " of commerce, appears to acquire a zealous big-brothership to the interests of financial equilibrium, that argues an exaggerated view of its importance to society in general.

Self-confusion in the author due to moral adulteration arises either through a self-contradictory use of words—words for instance *defined* strictly scientifically and then used with a moral tone ; or arises in the course of a deductive reasoning when scientific deduction is mixed with moral implication. So important are these two sources of error that to each a separate section will be devoted.

§ 6

SELF-CONFUSION IN THE
USE OF WORDS

Economists have set out to define the demand for an article as the amount of it people want or crave and are able to purchase at a given price. If prices vary on the market the demand varies, i.e. the amounts sold and purchased at each different price vary. But these variations are ascertainable and could probably be stated by an expert in the particular market concerned without fear of contradiction from others " in the know ". How much x was or would be sold on the market at price y is the sort of question we should not be surprised to see asked on a government form ; nor should we be surprised if the question was to be answered " to the best of a man's ability " on oath. It is the sort of question to which the same answer within fairly narrow limits may be expected from all experienced observers.

UPLIFT IN ECONOMICS

The economist's original definition or
label of demand is thus designed to
indicate objectively measurable statements, that are independent of each
observer's peculiar feelings and sentiments, and that can be put in fairly exact
terms of price and amount bought or
sold on the market.

Now the label " demand " by excluding
all but such exact objective information
has obtained an enviable reputation ; like
the signature of some reputable firm
which has been attached only to the most
upright of dealings, it has acquired
prestige, and the economist who is also
a propagandist is sooner or later tempted
to use its hall-mark for his special propaganda.

Under stress of enthusiasm in some
ethical argument there seems to be a
peculiar temptation to use the word
demand (the amount a man is craving
and able to purchase at a given price)
to refer to wants (what a man is craving
to purchase *if* he were able to pay the
price) and even to refer to needs (what
a man *ought* to be craving to purchase).

USE OF WORDS

This interchange of words that are supposed to refer to different things, inevitably leads to the identification by reader and by author of the different things themselves ; a confusion very evident when speaking of the different characteristics of any commodity that may arouse or satisfy demands, wants, and needs, respectively. The characteristic of being demanded, what Professor Taussig wisely distinguishes by the word vendibility, is confusedly identified with the characteristic of being wanted (the economist's " utility ") and with the characteristic of being needed, that is, of being, in the author's moral judgment, beneficial or desirable to the individual or society.

This identification of vendibility, utility, and sheer " beneficence ", and the corresponding indentification of demands, wants and needs, has led Mr. H. D. Henderson into a most attractive argument for the present " price " system, as no worse than a system where one may " suppose all the difficulties of human perversity and administrative technique to have been surmounted and a wise, disinterested executive to be in supreme control of our business life ".

The argument is that where two articles such as mutton and wool are produced jointly, the number of sheep required for clothing a normal family in wool, " allowing for differences in climate, and possibly indulging somewhat the caprices of human taste ", and the number of sheep required for mutton, would tally even remotely only by an extraordinary coincidence.[1] Hence the wise disinterested executive would be driven back to the present monetary system selling both mutton and wool at a price, and adjusting their respective prices up or down until the consumption of the two things were in the required ratio. But if the executive, writes

[1] That is, supposing the proportion of wool to meat cannot be varied ; a rigidity which is in fact untrue. Different breeds of sheep yield different proportions as Henderson points out, but this is a trifling matter compared to the possibility (which economists habitually over-look) of slaughtering sheep earlier or later in life and thus getting fewer or more clips per carcase.

USE OF WORDS

Henderson, " acted in this manner, what essentially would it be doing? It would be seeking by deliberate contrivance to reproduce, in respect of this particular problem, the very conditions which occur to-day without aim or effort on the part of anyone at all ".

This argument we are told " does not show the folly of Socialism or the superiority of Laissez-faire. What it does show is the existence in the economic world of an order more profound and more permanent than any of our social schemes, and equally applicable to them all ". And what does Mr. Henderson's " order " refer to? " What, then, might we expect to find if order was non-existent in the economic world? Surely that some things such as wool would be produced in quantities many times in excess of the demand for them, quite possibly five, ten, or twenty times in excess ; while conversely the supplies of others such as mutton might fall far short of what was required. But in practice we find nothing of the sort. Somehow it comes about that an equilibrium is established between the demand for and the supply of every commodity ".[1]

But surely a wise, disinterested executive would aim at supplying people's wants or, better still, their needs, not their demand. Substituting the original definition for the word " demand ", the last sentence quoted runs " Somehow it comes about that an equilibrium is established between the amount of a commodity people are craving for *and able to purchase at the given price* and the supply of every commodity "—an " order " that fails to stir enthusiasm or to appeal as one that wise executives should " contrive to reproduce ". Rich men may needlessly demand, i.e. offer money in exchange, for things that poor men need but have not the purchase-money to demand, as Henderson, later on admits ;[2] and even if all persons were equally wealthy a wise executive would

[1] H. D. Henderson, *Supply and Demand*, pp. 8-11.

[2] Chapter III, § 6. " The amounts of money which different people are prepared to pay for different consumers' goods are no reliable indication of the real utilities, the amounts of human satisfaction which they yield ".

not necessarily tie itself down to providing people with what they craved at the expense of what they needed.

It appears as though Henderson had confused not only his readers but himself by substituting in the course of his pleading, terms with exact but limited references, for terms, like requirement and order, that are undefined and often morally coloured. Requirement may refer to a need, a craving, or a demand ; and when using this word the author may easily be changing from the moral or optative to the scientific or indicative mood without noticing the change himself. The order which *a wise disinterested executive* would seek " by deliberate contrivance to reproduce " is an ethical ideal where the needs or possibly the wants and cravings of people would be paramount. The order where the words *demand* and *supply* are at all relevant is the actual price-system of here and to-day—not necessarily such a profound and universally prevalent order, either.

Economists cannot have it both ways.

UPLIFT IN ECONOMICS

They must either confine themselves to measurable classes of fact like demand, the satisfaction of which is not of ultimate importance to a wise control of life ; or if they wish to deal with ultimate good or to appeal to the exuberant imaginations of their pupils, they must abandon all pretensions to accurate measurement.

In the present state of knowledge an author's use of accurate indicative terms in what is, by implication, an ethical manner, tends to confuse not only his readers but himself into the bargain. The constant soaring ambition of economists to lay down laws in precise terms about man's requirements, needs, and welfare, lies at the root of at least half the criticism levelled at current economic doctrine by political scientists and other publicists. The following passage is Prof. Hobhouse's presumably fair summary of the claims made by Mr. Henderson in an address on the " Implications of the Cambridge School of Economists " to a London audience.[1]

" Given freedom of mobility, a trans-

[1] *Economics*, November, 1924.

ference of industrial energies will take place, till the fullest value with the least waste in the circumstances of the case is obtained from each factor. The result of this transference is then to secure a larger total of general satisfaction. Thus the principle is not only comprehensive and consistent but socially advantageous. That is to say it is just, it gives to all fair value, fairness being what works out to the maximum benefit of all ".

In this quotation *value* and *satisfaction* are taken as more or less identical with socially advantageous, just, fair, and beneficial to all; and definite economic concepts are again mixed up with ethical value. Professor Hobhouse has little difficulty in exposing the absurd results of this confusion between Social Value, where Value is used in the sense of what is conducive to moral good (e.g. general happiness according to some), and Competitive Value, where Value is used definitely as Exchange-Value or Price.

"Even for the individual the repeated satisfaction of a number of passing desires is not the way of enduring happiness.

57

UPLIFT IN ECONOMICS

Still less do the aggregate satisfactions
of a number of selfish individuals add up
to a sum which is the happiness of the
whole. Stated in terms of satisfaction
the National Dividend is a polite but
unscientific fiction ".

But Professor Hobhouse, though aware
of the absurd and distressing symptoms,
does not diagnose the disease or suggest
the remedy. The first step is to purge
economic theory of all discussions of
social justice, fairness, *true* happiness,
real satisfaction, individual merits . . . .
and to reserve certain words to indicate
observable and, if possible, measurable
facts and characteristics of the economic
situation. Among such words I would
list demand and vendibility (the
characteristic of being demanded), want
and utility (the characteristic of being
wanted), supply and costs,[1] as well as
exchange-value. The word welfare on
the other hand seems to me too far gone
in ethical adulteration for salvage pur-

[1] An attempt to formulate the exact reference
of these words will be found in my *Economics
and Human Behaviour*.

58

USE OF WORDS

poses. It does not wholly refer to
observable fact but depends partly on
the observer's own opinion of right and
wrong conduct.[1]

[1] Prof. Pigou defines welfare as consisting
" in that group of satisfactions and dissatis-
factions which can be brought into relation
with a money measure ", and thus intends the
word to refer to what men can be observed to
want or crave, and to get or not to get. But
Hobson is nearer the general use of the word
(*Freethought in the Social Sciences*, p. 168) as
a " single word to express both what man is
after and what he ought to be after ".

§ 7

SELF-CONFUSION
IN DEDUCTIVE REASONING

Confusion of the author by his own moral implications is greatly facilitated by authors' peculiar method of reasoning about social phenomena. It might be supposed that the facts and events would first be thoroughly ascertained and general conclusions drawn, before an interpretation and explanation were hazarded. But this is not the orthodox method. It is usual to start out with general presumptions about human nature, that it invariably seeks pleasure and avoids pain, buys cheap and sells dear, loves freedom and never will be slaves, etc., and to *deduce* the course of events from this presumption, often by the orthodox logical syllogism. The presumption about human nature is in fact the major premiss and the conclusions " follow " to the tune of the adverb *presumably,*

DEDUCTIVE REASONING

instead of being laboriously sifted from observations at first only to be taken as *apparently* true.

The theory of economics affords the most perfect instance of the use of the deductive method in social research. From general presumptions made about human nature, principles of economics are deduced and from these principles further corollaries and sub-principles. But the word principle, which is such a favourite in the titles of economic text-books, is also used for the optative premiss of the "practical syllogism" and for any practical deduction that may in turn become an optative.[1] And the words natural and normal have also been applied to ideal states of affairs interference with which (e.g. by government) is, almost by definition, wrong. It is a *principle* of Economics that exchange value in the long run tends to equal cost of production ; but it is also a *principle* that one ought not to give money to unknown beggars. One is a principle in the indicative mood from which indicative

[1] Above § 1.

conclusions may be drawn, the other an optative ethical principle of right and wrong ; but unfortunately the two get mixed up and the ethical principle may appear in the guise of the indicative principle, to play the role of the major premiss in the deductive argument with devastating effect.

The same is true of the word law. A law of economics (or political science) is "a statement that a certain course of action may be expected under certain conditions from the members of a social group ",[1] but there are also the more familiar laws of a State that (imperatively) prohibit certain courses of action. The same confusion between an indicative statement, if it is a deduction, and an imperative command, is also manifested in the use of the auxiliary verb " ought ". A doctor may be overheard saying that a patient of his *ought*, scientifically speaking, to have died but in fact lived, and in economics we often read statements such as " the yield on consols is pushed up relatively to the yield on bills more

[1] Marshall, *Principles of Economics*, I, iii, § 4.

than it *ought to be* ".[1] What " ought to be " is in this context the deduction that follows indicatively (though often regardless of actual facts) from the premisses that were selected, not necessarily a socially desirable consummation.

This interchange of terms in the language of logical deductions and in that of moral precepts is confusing enough, but there is a further terminological source of confusion in the device of hypostatization.

An hypostasis is a metaphysically conceived underlying substance, and the word hypostatization may be used to refer to the practice of supposing a force or substance to exist though not directly observable by the human senses. The Real Presence or Subsistence of Persons or Spirits is imagined whose conduct infallibly follows (indicative mood) the principles of right or (e.g. the Devil) wrong. Or a " right-thinking " moral people may be presupposed who invari-

---

[1] Pigou (quoting F. Lavington), *Industrial Fluctuations*, p. 252.

UPLIFT IN ECONOMICS

ably obey some moral law.[1] The way
is then clear to deduce from this major
premise all manner of sub-principles,
minor laws and bye-laws on the most
approved logical lines.

Prohibition of the employment of little
boys to sweep out chimneys was repeatedly
urged in Parliament between 1817 and
1819, but reforms of this kind, replied
Lord Lauderdale, could be left " entirely
to the moral feelings of perhaps the most
moral people on the face of the earth ".
In 1853 this presumption still held the
field and Lord Clancarty opined that it
was not " characteristic of the British
nation to disregard the appeal of
humanity ".[2]

Concurrently with the enunciation of
these presumptions, particular, observable,
events appeared to be occurring at specific
times and places.[3]

" It was stated in one case, tried by
the Hull magistrates, in 1848, that a

---

[1] Or happily agree with the author. See Woodrow
Wilson, *History of the American People, passim.*
[2] Mr. and Mrs. Hammond, *Lord Shaftesbury,*
pp. 218, 223.
[3] *Op. cit.* pp. 221, 222.

THE AUDIENCE DISTRACTED

Dr. Marshall's readers. The dictum that " a woman may display wealth, but she may not display only her wealth, by her dress ; or else she defeats her ends "[1] might be welcome in the latest handbook of étiquette for ladies, but it is liable to check a self-respecting economics student in her course of text-book reading. Nor would any struggling W.E.A. pupil see the necessity of a footnote to assure us that " there are many fine natures among domestic servants ".[2]

In the introduction to his *Industrial Fatigue in Relation to Output*, Professor Spooner goes even further and assures the unwitting that " no one who has been privileged to work with, to manage, or to teach the artisans of this country and who understands them and their psychology, could fail to have a profound respect for them. They are in the main sensible, intelligent men, and many of them who have made good use of their spare time are cultured and extremely well educated; indeed the late Mr.Mundella,

---

[1] *Principles of Economics*, 6th Ed., p. 88.
[2] *Op. cit.* p. 208.

29

UPLIFT IN ECONOMICS

when Vice-President of the Board of Education, said, at a prize distribution, that he knew many working men who would grace any gentleman's drawing room ".

The persistence of the class distinction and the peculiar monastic methods of bringing up the male young among the English well-to-do classes, makes English writers, the majority of whom are male and well-to-do, particularly liable to " put off " and distract their poorer and their feminine readers by moralizations, implications and innuendoes peculiar to their class and sex. They should be doubly anxious to avoid unnecessary excursions of a critical nature, whether condemnations or pats on the back.

Science transcends national boundaries and it is not wise therefore to confound and distract foreign readers by running completely counter to their point of view and to write (in an otherwise " indicatively " stated passage) of things as good or favourable or satisfactory that diminish the prosperity of their country relatively to that of the writer,

DEDUCTIVE REASONING

child of ten had been sold five times over. He was a clever worker, and though unable to walk, owing to his injuries, had cleaned no less than twelve chimneys the previous Saturday. At Nottingham, in 1850, a boy of ten, Samuel Whitt, was jammed in a chimney, below which a fire was smouldering. He was ultimately torn down by two people, standing one on top of the other, and died in agony a few hours later. In this case nobody was punished, for there was not even an inquest. On Christmas Eve that same year, in Manchester, Stephen Ratcliffe, aged eleven, was " accidentally suffocated in a heated flue ". So said the Coroner's jury, and there the matter ended. Next year, 1851, at Hunslet, near Leeds, George Wilson, aged ten, after sweeping nine chimneys, died in the tenth ".

At Manchester, in 1847, " a master sweep, John Gordon, was tried for the death of a boy of seven, named Thomas Price. The child was forced to go, for the second time, into a hot flue at Messrs. Tennant's chemical works ; he screamed and sobbed, but in vain, for the master

65

declared ' the young devil is foxing '.
Finally, he was taken out half asphyxiated,
thrown on straw, and cruelly beaten in
the hope that he might be beaten back
to consciousness. Soon after he died in
convulsions. A medical witness found
that death was due to convulsions produced by suffocation, and that there
were severe bruises ".

But it was the facts as they appeared,
not the comfortable presumption that
had to give way. The injuries inflicted
upon chimney boys in sending them up
chimneys were only apparent. British
morality being what it was, these injuries
presumably could not happen and did
not happen. The logic of this conclusion
can indeed be thrown into the form of a
formal deductive syllogism.

> No moral person would be the
> cause of injuries to chimney boys.

> The British are the most moral
> people on the face of the earth.

> Therefore British sweep masters
> or their (British) clients are not the
> cause of injuries to chimney sweeps.

DEDUCTIVE REASONING

It is the Moral British People that is here the hypostasis, the convenient fiction, figment or myth, which turns what is really a wish, or at best a mere opinion, into the major premiss (in the indicative mood) of an orthodox logical syllogism.

Similarly other people may be hypostasized as an immoral or sinful people. Bias is in fact particularly likely to chrystallize in comparing groups, into one of which the author must have been born and within which he must infallibly remain.

Race and sex bias, piquant as they are in literature, belles lettres, and conversation, are in scientific work a potent source of confusion between fact and fancy and an obstacle in achieving correct generalizations. Ellwood writes of the " degenerate strains of the oppressed peoples of Southern and Eastern Europe " and quotes the claim " that the Chinese are grossly immoral ",[1] and it is easy to infer that he is himself not of Slav or Chinese stock.   His reiterated attribution

[1] *Op. cit.* pp. 188, 192.

of superior culture to one particular race places him, in fact, genealogically.

Here the sociologist is undoubtedly confusing himself and vitiating his statement of fact. He objects to Chinamen on some score, e.g., that his standard of living is insufficient for white men, and this leads him to attribute other qualities connected in his mind by their common " sinfulness ", but not connected in fact. The Chinaman is notoriously moral in the very sense Ellwood seems to use the word, i.e. his family and sexual relations are very strictly circumscribed, and it is his very thrift and hard work that makes him a dangerous competitor to the white man.

If a people is immoral as a general premiss, various forms of immorality can easily be deduced, and the author is led to attribute *all* or *most* qualities which he happens to disapprove of to persons, activities or things who are observed to possess in fact only *some* of the disapproved qualities.

§ 8

THE LAST STATE OF THE
MORAL SCIENCES

With wide differences in their major
premisses and in the moral implication
of the words they use, the social sciences
worked out deductively by persons of
different race, sex, or class, will tend to
differ considerably in their conclusions.
The natural sciences have accustomed
us to expect one unique conclusion on
points of fact. We are not told that,
on the problem whether we are descended
from angels or monkeys, there is " much
to be said on both sides ", or that " we
must look to both sides of the question "
whether the earth is round or flat. And
" liberal " economists or sociologists who
present more than one conclusion and
take credit for being dispassionate or
non-partisan are, scientifically, simply
bi-partisan and multipassionate.

Like theology and metaphysical philosophy, economics and sociology generally

tend to split up into rival or quite unrelated schools of thought ; and though there are not as many conflicting economic systems as there are irreconcilable philosophers and religions, this deficiency may soon be rectified, if purely deductive methods persist and the facts are not observed and accurately described.

" Economic Principles " are written mainly by the well-to-do, ignorant of the condition of their poorer neighbours, and imbued with a moral outlook and a conception of sin in some respects peculiar to their station. As a result the more independent-minded among the poorer classes have come to distinguish orthodox " bourgeois " economics, represented by the many common factors in the Austrian and Cambridge Schools, from Socialist, Marxian or proletarian Economics ; and there is also the Single Tax Sect, the Historical School, and the followers of Ruskin, Morris, J. A. Hobson and Major Douglas, not to mention the believers in the Instincts.[1] If Economics were

[1] See Florence, *Economics and Human Behaviour*, § II.

really the science it sets out to be, though there might be temporary differences in interpretation, e.g., the differentia of Austrian and Cambridge Schools, there should not be in the long run two or more conflicting versions of its most elementary observations.[1] It would not be a question of what Marx said or wrote or meant to write, or what Ricardo, or Marshall said, wrote or meant to write, but how the facts themselves, not the Texts and Bibles about them, are to be interpreted.

Marxian Economics bears within itself unmistakable traces of a nascent theology. Scurrilous sceptics have permitted themselves to speak of a gospel according to St. Marx, and to compare the expectation of the social revolution to that of the Second-Coming, and even to parallel the

[1] Curiously, many of these different versions of Economics spring from the same traditional doctrine, much as the different religious systems of the world are found to have common ancestors. Marx deduced his schismatic theories very largely from Ricardo (of the true succession), and so did Henry George and the Single Tax heretics.   Are the deductions of the " orthodox " always liable to be capped by a fanatical super-structure of corollaries ?

mysteries of the generation of surplus value with those of the Immaculate Conception. The Capitalist is regarded as Satan responsible for all Sin and Evil, including wars, pestilences and scarcities.[1] These concordances are blasphemous, but they shed light on a numerous series of unorthodox economic fetishes and superstitions.

"Bourgeois" Economics does not indulge quite so flagrantly in hypostatization, though allusions to the Sacred laws of Supply and Demand, the Hidden Hand, the Eternal Basis[2] of Economic Science, Economic Harmonies, and an "all pervading uniformity and order", all approach metaphysical and theological conceptions rather dangerously. Unquestionably the orthodox treatment of the entrepreneur and his function should make a realist uneasy.

The bringing together and organizing of the various factors or agents of pro-

[1] Even Mr. and Mrs. Sidney Webb join in this hell-raising, cf. *Decay of Capitalism*, Chapters V and VI.

[2] De Quincey on Ricardo quoted by Keynes, *Scope and Method*, p. 297.

duction were seen to be a necessary activity in the economic world and an entrepreneur was assumed as a real person whose " function " it was so to create and organize. How far this hypostasis corresponds to any persons or sets of persons in actual fact, has recently been the subject of an interesting monograph by Mr. Maurice Dobb ;[1] but undoubtedly whether a fiction or based on fact, the myth of the entrepreneur and the so-called " entrepreneurial " function has been a useful dogma with which to *épater* the anti-bourgeois.

This imputation of a function in all things and moreover a function for Good is a practice familiar in the Sunday School and in popular theology generally. There is good in all things. The gadfly exists, and as he must have a useful function to perform, is it not that of moving cattle from pasture to pasture? And the man who is observed to make a profit is he not paid for and in proportion to his contribution,[2] his successful

[1] *Capitalist Enterprise and Social Progress*, Cf. esp. introductory remarks, pp. 5 and 6.
[2] Fetter, *Principles*, p. 291.

organization,[1] his productivity,[2] or his " superiority over less capable men with whom he is in competition " ?[3]

To say that a man's profits are determined by the difference in his efficiency from that of the man on the margin is not, as Mr. Dobb points out, to solve the problem. " It merely introduces the question : what is the cause of the scarcity of efficient undertakers which fixes the margin where it is ?. . . . For the margin is only where it is because of the scarcity of the supply of superior units."

But more important in Mr. Dobb's opinion than this " misapprehension about the importance of the margin " is the " ethical judgment that is usually implied by the manner of exposition ". The " contribution ", " organization ", " productivity ", " superiority " of the man who makes a profit is taken to be of moral benefit to the community, a Service to Society.

There is a particular implication, says

[1] Kirkaldy, *Wealth,* pp 137-8.
[2] J. B. Clark, *Distribution of Wealth,* pp. 8-9.
[3] Flux, *Economic Principles,* p. 153.

74

MORAL SCIENCES

Mr. Dobb,[1] which is surprisingly common in all economic thought and dominates the field of applied economics to an alarming extent.

"It is the conclusion which the theory of distribution is usually assumed to imply, that (with the possible exception of landowners and some *rentiers* and in the absence of 'economic friction') persons tend to secure an income in proportion to some 'service' which they contribute to society. This is the gist of Prof. Clark's productivity theory of distribution, epitomized in the statement . . . . that 'a natural law' tends to 'give to every agent of production the amount of wealth which that agent creates'. It is to be seen in such a typical statement as that of Sir J. A. R. Marriott, that since profit represents the skill of the person who 'runs' the concern, neither the wage-earner nor the consumer has any claim, economic or ethical, to any portion of this net profit".

"This Service Theory of distribution" continues Mr. Dobb, "seems to owe its

[1] *Op. cit.* p 147.

popularity to a loose usage of words. In one sense, of course, no payment can be obtained except for a service rendered to someone ; but this is not *more* than to say that you cannot charge more than the traffic will bear, or to say that there can be no value without utility. In this sense the most extortionate usurer or monopolist is getting no more than the ' service ' he is rendering ; but it does not follow that his payment is in *proportion* to the ' service ' he renders. Generally, however, the Service Theory is made a corollary from the fact that payments are made to agents of production according to the *marginal* service contributed. But since institutions play a large part in determining where the margin is—e.g., by restricting the supply of some services and by enabling some persons to supply more of a given service than others—the corollary should really be that an agent tends to be remunerated according to the marginal service which *existing social institutions permit or enable it to render*. Amended in this way, the statement loses most of

MORAL SCIENCES

its original meaning ; at any rate it loses its force as an ethical judgment ".

Political scientists themselves admit that " Political Economy existed before modern Sociology was born and is still the only part of it which is obviously and indisputably successful as a science of explanation ".[1] And the science of politics has certainly suffered more severely than economics from implication in moral issues. For this there are at least two peculiar reasons.

(a) Political Science has hitherto dealt mainly with the conduct of the central State-Government, and the particular government of the day offers a visible bull's eye for the shafts of the more practical of political thinkers. Governments are a definite body of persons with recognized power to change or maintain conditions, with whom it is worth while arguing the rights and wrongs of things. Panaceas are likely to be freely offered when there is one duly constituted body of practitioners to apply them.

[1] Bosanquet, *The Philosophical Theory of the State*, p. 27.

77

UPLIFT IN ECONOMICS

And sometimes the political practitioners, feeling unduly prominent in the public eye, are grateful for commendation of their doctoring or of the system that constituted them doctors. Even the classics of political science when they imply moral judgment are accused of apologetics or tendenciousness, unconscious perhaps, but none the less, illegitimate in scientific exposition. The relations of John Locke to the English Revolution, of Hegel to the Prussian monarchy, even of Sidgwick himself to the Victorian Constitution are all suspect as " rationalizations " after the event. Hypostatization is a frequent device, Rousseau's myth of the State of Nature and the Social Contract being the leading case. Most of these " thinkers " certainly got things done or undone or prevented things being done or undone as far as the local and contemporary situation went, but much of their thinking is not in the scientific indicative mood and cannot be used generally or applied in any other (e.g., our present) situation.

MORAL SCIENCES

(*b*) There has always been a conscious tradition dating at least from Aristotle, that political science should deal with the morals of political behaviour. Sidgwick declares in the first chapter of his *Elements of Politics* " we must determine what ought to be so far as the Constitution and action of government are concerned, as distinct from what is or has been ".

There is of course no reason why people should not devote themselves (if they have the means, time and inclination) to this sort of philosophy and metaphysic of politics, but such a discipline cannot take the place of an " indicative " political science. Some people must devote themselves whole-heartedly to the discovery of the various causes and effects of political behaviour of various sorts without bothering about the rectitude or sinfulness of such behaviour ; so that (apart from the sheer interest of knowing the truth) *whatever* effect is desired as as end, it may be produced by bringing about the discovered causes as means to that end.

UPLIFT IN ECONOMICS

It is a life's work to contribute merely to the discovery of the forces actually at work in a political society. And just as the physicist or the chemist devotes himself solely to such discovery, leaving the invention of the means of using these forces to others ; similarly some political scientists must resign themselves to the acting of one rôle, to specialization in one function. What ought to be the constitution and action of government depends on what is considered the good of society. We cannot embark on a practical policy without first judging some purpose to be good. Practice must depend on moral outlook, the Imperative on the Optative desired. But as a matter of fact what the good of Society is, has not *yet* been settled. Jeremy Bentham and the Utilitarians proclaimed it was the Happiness of the Majority of people. But since this allows the complacent to sit tight and say " the poor are quite happy in their slums, why disturb them ? ", volumes have had to be written to explain or explain away the meaning of happiness or to advocate the substitution of other

MORAL SCIENCES

ideals.[1] Is the last state of Political Science to be a cockpit of moral emotions?

[1] For a summary see Graham Wallas, *Great Society*, Chapter VII.

§ 9

SCIENTIFIC AMORALITY

To demonstrate that it is not merely desirable but possible to write economics, political science and sociology generally, in the spirit and letter of the indicative mood, the works of modern anthropologists may be compared with the writings of some, perhaps old-fashioned, missionaries.

Both may be describing the same customs among the same tribe ; but while the missionary in question has turned his shocked eyes upon the nakedness and the impropriety of his prospective converts . . . . and can only suggest further knitting efforts among the ladies back home and the introduction of a more seemly ritual at the front, the anthropologist avoids being shocked and passing moral judgments as far as he can and proceeds to record and interpret the strange facts he meets, with composure, in the indicative mood.

SCIENTIFIC AMORALITY

In his Autobiography, the Rev. James Paton tells us he " found the Tannese to be painted Savages, enveloped in all the superstitions and wickedness of Heathenism. All the men and children go in a state of nudity. The older women wear grass skirts, and the young women and girls grass or leaf aprons like Eve in Eden. They are exceedingly ignorant, vicious, and bigoted and almost void of natural affection ".

Compare the description of the same Tannese by C. B. Humphreys[1]. Their " superstitions " and " wickedness " in the form of " myths and traditions ", circumcision ceremonies, initiation dances and even cannibalism are described without ill-feeling, and their clothing—or the lack of it—accurately but calmly noted under " Domestic Conditions ", together with housing conditions, food and its preparation and recreation. As for the character of the Tannese, their " emotions " (which " seem to show a greater similarity to our own than is

[1] C. B. Humphreys, *The Southern New Hebrides*, 1926.

83

usually admitted ") are " observed and recorded whenever any occurrence throws light on the subject ". Throughout the book there is no stigmatization even when discussing sex-habits ; a possible exception, when the island is said to have a " clean " record in the matter of sexual perversion, merely proving the rule.

The social enquirer of to-day is still in the shocked missionary stage. He is wrapped in the atmosphere of Animal Stories, Reading Without Tears, or Little Arthur's History of England where, if my memory serves me, the principal basis for judging each king's policy is his conjugal fidelity and sexual habits generally. Why should the social enquirer not devote himself to the habits and institutions of his own time and race, as the anthropologist, the ethnologist, and the archaeologist are doing for other places, other races and other times ? Numerous social phenomena at home seem to offer a fruitful field for the collection, accurate measurement, comparison, and generalisation of facts in the purely indicative mood.

SCIENTIFIC AMORALITY

To engage the interest of the audience there is no need to whip them into moral indignation " at " people's behaviour or to stir them to the espousal of a " Cause ". The mere existence and relationships of many contemporary social phenomena are surely of sufficient interest : the mating habits of the " lower orders," for instance, with their consecutive stages of having a " follower ", " keeping company ", " walking out ", " courting " ; the organization and localization—the haunts and habits—of literary Bohemians ; female fashions, their origin, spread, trend, and periodicity ; le snobisme ; manners and instincts of the sporting gentleman ; etc., etc. All these subjects have furnished food for sermons ; but could they not also prove matter for scientific enquiry ? Modern novelists, particularly H. G. Wells, Arnold Bennett, and Sinclair Lewis have certainly managed to describe social conditions, institutions, habits, rules of etiquette and good form and so forth, without taking moral attitudes about them.

If the economist, and social enquirer

generally, feels that the customs he is
describing are too close to him to pass
without comment, let him record the
facts as facts (not as texts for sermons)
and give vent to his indignation, horror,
or admiration at another time or in
another place. Or if there must be
continuous patter to satisfy the author's
or feed the reader's sense of sin let it
be clearly understood as *Obiter Dicta*,
and printed, if necessary, in a different
type or colour, say praise in blue, con-
demnation in red. " If moral judgments
are expressed or practical applications
pointed out " writes Dr. Keynes " they
should be regarded as digressions, not as
economic dicta constituting integral and
essential portions of economic science
itself ".

Many leading economists have indeed
recognized the need, if they wrote in more
than one mood, of separating off these
various moods by assigning to each a
different place in their works. Malthus
felt strongly enough about the limitation
of families and has some beautiful passages
in praise of " the exercise of virtue " ;

SCIENTIFIC AMORALITY

but this did not prevent him reviewing fairly dispassionately in the first two books of his Essay " the Checks to Population in the Less Civilized Parts of the World and in Past Times ", and drawing General Conclusions (Book II, Chap. XIII),[1] before proceeding to discuss, in his third book, " The Different Systems or Expedients which have been Proposed or Have Prevailed in Society, as they affect the Evils arising from the Principle of Population ". His own view " of Moral Restraint, and our Obligation to practise this Virtue " is not fully developed till the fourth and last book of his Essay.

Turning to more recent economists, Professor Pigou's *Industrial Fluctuations* provides a model arrangement. Part I is entitled *Causation* and its twenty-two chapters are written throughout in the indicative mood to the exclusion of all moral implications. Part II is entitled *Remedies*. The introductory first chapter

[1] Though Malthus' use of the word " Vice " (in the first two books) as one of the positive checks is certainly confusing. He seems to have realized this. Cf. footnote Book I, ch. II.

87

discusses whether the popular opinion that industrial fluctuations as such must be social evils, is valid or invalid. Here in fact is a deliberate discussion of the optative step of the " practical syllogism ". Professor Pigou comes to the conclusion that, under modern industrial conditions, the fluctuations with which he is dealing *are* evils, and in the remaining chapters of Part II he discusses the various ways of preventing or palliating them that have been publicly set forth in the imperative mood.

The deliberate exclusion of the moral or optative mood in the scientific portion of a book does not imply that the author must cut himself off from helping to improve the lot of mankind. Professor Pigou himself records his appreciation of " Comte's great phrase " " It is for the heart to suggest our problems ; it is for the intellect to solve them . . . The only position for which the intellect is primarily adapted is to be the servant of the social sympathies ". But the amoral attitude and practice of the anthropologists and leading economists that

SCIENTIFIC AMORALITY

have just been quoted may so shock my more idealistic and constructively-minded readers that I must conclude, in my epilogue, with some account of the way this sociology without sin may co-operate in social reconstruction.

§ 10. EPILOGUE

A PLAN OF PRACTICAL
CO-OPERATION

The discussion and judgment of what acts of men lift upwards, what acts of men are socially wrong or socially right, is not to be abandoned, but—according to my thesis—should form the subject of a moral philosophy or social ethics consciously set apart from the *science* of sociology, economics or politics. Once social philosophy or ethics is confused by an author with social science there results the possible self-confusion of the author himself, and the almost certain misleading and distraction of his audience. Though the statement or implication that some act leads to uplift has the appearance of indicating a fact, yet uplift has no systematically interpretable reference established by scientific usage or legal precedent, or laid down by statute. The author may vary in his sense of

PRACTICAL CO-OPERATION

uplift from time to time and context to context ; and an audience may have conceptions of uplift that differ from individual to individual, all of them differing from the conceptions of the author. Hence a social science thinking in terms of uplift, is a Babel of distracting, misleading and self-confusing schemes, where hope must forever be deferred of the ordered progress to which the natural sciences have accustomed us in their step by step discovery of truth.

A re-organization of thought and action is thus implied. Economists and political scientists generally will become specialists surveying *amorally* in indicative mood the wide varieties of human behaviour, the positive and negative reactions of human beings. They will trace the result of one reaction or stimulus on another and discover how consequences can be produced and prevented. They will be fact-finders, not fault-finders, and will not be called upon to judge what particular reactions or what specific consequences are good and what are bad. Ethical judgment will be left to philoso-

phers meditating in optative mood upon
the nature of good behaviour and *mis*-
behaviour and viewing reactions negative
and positive as contingent sins of omission
and commission. Thus the practical
reformer will order affairs in imperative
mood with clear knowledge of cause
and consequence and full realization of
good and evil. His policy will at last
be both scientific and right.

This specialization in each of the
three moods of the practical syllogism
is necessitated by the brevity of human
life and the limits of individual effort.
But it is also called for, like all division
of labour, by the differences in people's
abilities and emotional make-up. An
intellect like Francis Bacon's is not
necessarily the most suitable for inspiring
people with " moral " desires, nor yet
for commanding practical measures to
lead them in that direction. " For
myself ", he writes, " I found that I was
fitted for nothing so well as for the study
of Truth ; as having a mind nimble and
versatile enough to catch the resemblance
of things (which is the chief point), and

at the same time steady enough to fix and distinguish their subtler differences; as being gifted by nature with desire to seek, patience to doubt, fondness to meditate, slowness to assert, readiness to reconsider, carefulness to dispose and set in order; and as being a man that neither affects what is new nor admires what is old and that hates every kind of imposture. So I thought my nature had a kind of familiarity and relationship with Truth ".

The way in which the " natural " economist or political scientist, the " familiar " of economic and political truth, *can* serve moral ends, consists in concentrating upon and perfecting the knowledge of facts and forces, their causes and results, as an instrument for bringing about practical policy *whatever* results are desired as optative ends.

Deliberate policy as we have said depends on an indicative or scientific, and an optative or moral " premiss ". Working alone economists and political experts can think out a " scientific " policy for the practical man in the sense of an *effective* policy that produces successfully whatever he desires. But if they work in co-operation with social reformers and public-spirited philanthropists who can feel and can express themselves adequately, in the optative mood, they may achieve a constructive policy that is both scientific and right. This is my plan :—a division of labour corresponding to the steps of the practical syllogism.

Against this plan it is often maintained that specialization in optative mood is unnecessary ; that there are many immediate ends, consciously expressed or not, that all experienced and public-spirited people will agree upon. The scientific enquirer may take these ends for granted, therefore, and speak of his scientific policies, that effect these ends by producing their causes and conditioning factors, as right and good. He will thereby shorten his sentences and interest all people of goodwill (including himself perhaps) in his work. People agree that death rates ought to be kept down, and therefore the right policy is assuredly to keep drains and drinking water apart.

PRACTICAL CO-OPERATION

People agree that knowledge ought to be handed on, and therefore the right policy is assuredly to maintain schools. People are also found to agree that well-to-do couples who can afford it ought to have at least a certain number of children ; and many other commonly accepted desiderata occur especially where the objective is limited and subordinate, like killing the fly in the illustrative practical syllogism.

But this " short circuiting " of all independent discussion of the optatives desired is a dangerous ambition for the scientific expert, whether undertaken for publicity purposes or as a bona fide moral crusade. In discussing practical policies, it will always be safer to indicate the precise measure of any " good " that is mentioned, such as lower death rates ; for in social affairs innumerable optative goods find mention that are either not clear, or are clearly in conflict, and that must, in the imperative stage, lead to different practical policies.

Should a village tax itself nineteen

shillings in the pound to instal a model drainage system? The optative of a possibly slightly lower death rate is here in conflict with that of a certainly lower standard of comfort among rate-payers. If schools are to be maintained, the practical question what kind of school to maintain must depend upon whether the superior intelligence of the few *or* the diffusion of culture among the many is the optative in view. If a high rate of children per rich family is to be preached, is this because the richer is also considered the cleverer stock, or simply to bring about a greater population generally? If the former is the, perhaps sub-conscious, optative there is the alternate policy of educating the poorer children that are born, to be cleverer; if the latter is the immediate optative, the ultimate " super-ordinate " optative is involved whether it is the maximum happiness per head that is wanted or the maximum aggregate of happiness. If the National Dividend is £3,000,000,000 a year would it be best if there were **four** million well-to-do individuals with

PRACTICAL CO-OPERATION

£750 a year each, or forty million poorly off at £75 a year?[1]

The greatest happiness of the greatest number is only one of many ultimate goods suggested by moral philosophers, and it is necessary for scientists who wish to co-operate, to discover not only the things that produce happiness, but everything that may produce any other ideal that may be held. Moreover, since it is impossible to tell what will produce any of these suggested " goods " till it has been tried by observation or experiment, science must try all things heedless of the latest theories of good. Thus whatever the latest theory about good, the knowledge the science has acquired may be used to further the particular " good " of that theory.

The science of economics shows, for instance, that low wages are often due to ignorance of the labourer as to where

---

[1] Similarly a cricket expert may be puzzled whether to consider a man a better batter if he has made 1,000 runs in 40 completed innings and thus shows an average 25, or if he has only made 300 runs in ten completed innings but with the higher average of 30.

UPLIFT IN ECONOMICS

high wages could be secured, or his inability to travel to any region of high wages. So the practical politician secures the " good " of high wages by building an Employment Exchange where the labourer can be told where to find high wages and given means to reach that place. But on the other hand many people deep down in their inner drawing-room or club life believe that labourers should be paid less; "the lower classes drink their money away so terribly you know ". The science of economics is always ready : a rise in wages is due partly to the competition of employers for hands. So the practical man federates employers. Science is open, to be used by all comers. Whatever result is wanted by anyone, science should know the factors producing it.

Does the monopolist want to get the largest income possible in the long run ? Economists will draw him charts to show the exact point on the demand curve where maximum net profit is squeezable out of the consumer and where traffic will " bear " the greatest exploitation ;

PRACTICAL CO-OPERATION

or social psychology may teach him by
means of advertizements and scientific
salesmanship to create a bigger and
better demand.

Does the State government want to
get the highest possible return from the
taxation of given luxuries? The political
economist will point to the varying
elasticity of demand of different commod-
ities and predict the yields of given
increases in the rates accordingly.

Does the Bolshevik Shop Steward
want a General or Particular Strike?
He may glean from economics that
strikes are more successful generally
in the boom phase of the business cycle,
among particular trades in joint demand
with others,[1] when undertaken for a
specific purpose,[2] and in industries
thoroughly trade-unionized.[3]

Is political democracy to be preferred
to individual liberty, representative
government to administrative efficiency,
justice and the prevention of crime to

[1] Marshall, *Principles of Economics*, V, vi, § 7.
[2] Moore, *Laws of Wages*, p. 124.
[3] Moore, *op. cit.* pp. 108-116.

the satisfaction of humanitarian senti-
ment ? These ideal conditions can seldom
all exist together, there is no one set of
factors from which they will all result,
and moral philosophers, enthusiasts, and
statesmen must be left to thrash out the
ideal optative. But whatever the optative, the connected and conditioning
facts, tendencies, and causes are discover-
able by the same method, to whatever
use the discoveries are subsequently put.

If those who are skilled in these methods
of research sum up their findings in the
indicative mood they will save over-
lapping and confusion. They may in
other capacities express their wishes and
recommendations, or they may leave their
findings to be applied by others. But
in either case—and this is the conclusion
—let there be an independent body of
knowledge of social affairs as there is in
the physical sciences, to be freely used
by social inventors or social innovators
in the interest of any optative whatsoever.

For Product Safety Concerns and Information please contact our EU
representative GPSR@taylorandfrancis.com Taylor & Francis Verlag GmbH,
Kaufingerstraße 24, 80331 München, Germany

Printed and bound by CPI Group (UK) Ltd, Croydon, CR0 4YY
13/05/2025
01869684-0001